Frank Wakeley Gunsaulus

Songs of Night and Day

Frank Wakeley Gunsaulus

Songs of Night and Day

ISBN/EAN: 9783743303713

Manufactured in Europe, USA, Canada, Australia, Japa

Cover: Foto ©Thomas Meinert / pixelio.de

Manufactured and distributed by brebook publishing software (www.brebook.com)

Frank Wakeley Gunsaulus

Songs of Night and Day

SONGS OF NIGHT AND DAY

BY

FRANK W. GUNSAULUS

CHICAGO
A. C. McCLURG AND COMPANY
1896

CONTENTS.

THE PASSING OF TENNYSON	11
LOVE'S TIDE	14
LINES READ AT THE FUNERAL SERVICES OF EUGENE FIELD	16
MIRABEAU	23
ON LOOKING OUT OF THE WINDOW OF EMERSON'S LIBRARY	24
SONNET ON BRITON RIVIERE'S PAINTING "DANIEL'S ANSWER TO THE KING"	25
ON THE DUCHESS SFORZA WITH THE STOLEN CAST OF THE HEAD OF DANTE	26
ON THE RECESSION OF THE FALLS OF NIAGARA	27
AT BEACH ST. MARY	28
ERYTHEIA	30
THE UNVANISHED EROS	35
ON A FELLOW PASSENGER ASLEEP ON THE TRAIN, WITH THE POEMS OF BION AND MOSCHUS IN HIS HANDS	37
ON HEARING OF WILLIAM WATSON'S ILLNESS	39

CONTENTS

ON THE FRAGMENTS OF SAPPHO'S POEMS IN THE EGYPTIAN MUSEUM AT BERLIN	42
A POET'S DREAM OF BELATED LOVE	45
HARVEST AND HOPE	47
AFTER READING SIR EDWIN ARNOLD'S VERSES	50
TO A DAWNING TALENT	52
ON MOREAU'S PICTURE: "MAIDEN WITH THE HEAD OF ORPHEUS"	55
THE POET AND THE SOLDIER	58
THE SUN SHALL BE NO MORE THY LIGHT BY DAY; NEITHER FOR BRIGHTNESS SHALL THE MOON GIVE LIGHT UNTO THEE	60
SIR PHILIP SIDNEY	62
EARLY MORNING AT PLYMOUTH	65
POETRY AND MUSIC	67
THE PURITAN	69
LOST IDEALS	71
THE CENTENARY OF JOHN KEATS	74
WAKING DREAMS	86
CARE AND CARELESSNESS	88
AT SANTA BARBARA	91
A WORD OF FAITH	93
SEA FOAM	95
CHRISTMAS, 1895	96
A SONG OF WIND AND RAIN	98
A BOAT SONG	100

CONTENTS

BISMARCK	102
SKY AND SEA	103
THE NAME OF GOD	105
INSOMNIA	107
LOVE AND IMMORTALITY	108
A BALLAD OF SPAIN	111
THE PERPETUAL WOOING	114
BETWEEN SUMMER AND WINTER	117
WHEN THE POET COMES	119
THE COMING PARADISE	121
ARCADY	124
ONE NIGHT AFTERWARD	126
TWO TRANSMIGRATIONS	129

"How far from Sinai, in earth's measured time,
    Riseth Parnassus?" once a minstrel asked.
The striking bells of ages in sweet chime
    Answered the poet in the pilgrim masked:—

"From flame-lit cliffs to summits white with snow,"
    They said;—"from rhythmic Truth's law-giving hour
To rhythmic Beauty's haunts where myrtles blow.
    Both peaks were lifted by one thrill of power."

Then, troubled sore that neither here nor there
    Were all earth's discords in pure concord held,
The minstrel-pilgrim, singing in his prayer,
    Sought Him whose power was love in times of eld.

"Beyond Parnassus riseth Calvary,"
    God said. "Leave thou Apollo's lyric morn;
Thence fare from Delphi to Gethsemane
    Where near the olives Love is crowned with thorn."

SONGS OF NIGHT AND DAY.

THE PASSING OF TENNYSON.

"On the bed lay a figure of breathing marble, flooded and bathed in the light of the full moon which streamed through an oriel window, his hand clasping a copy of Shakespeare he had asked for recently, and which he kept by him to the end. The moonlight, the majestic figure as he lay there drawing a thicker breath, irresistibly brought to our minds his own 'Passing of King Arthur.'"—*London Times*.

WITH Shakespeare's voice to guide him
   Where never ills betide him,
     Our poet sleeping went.
With rose-leaves softly falling,
   Through autumn echoes calling,
     He passed with soul attent.

Sad moon, o'er brown hills gleaming,
   Disturb not thou his dreaming;
     Thy singer silent lies.

SONGS OF NIGHT AND DAY

From moonlight, night, and wonder,
 He stepped to sunlight yonder—
  The poet's paradise.

His lyre-strings sweet and golden
 Are yet with music holden—
  Soft-echoed minstrelsy.
Shall ever English nation
 Forget her consecration
  Within his melody?

And if some tuneless singer,
 Or sorrowful light-bringer,
  Forget his song or way,—
This lyre with string unbroken
 Will ring, like music spoken,
  And tremble toward God's day.

He knew what scents are sweetest.
 His roses may be fleetest
  In poet's garden-song;

SONGS OF NIGHT AND DAY

Yet on his page they brighten;
    Their fragrant splendors lighten
        Life's pathway drear and long.

Bright bees will find sweet honey,
    When flower-bells fresh and sunny
        Encrimson hills and vales;
And darkened souls woe-stricken
    Will feel slain hopes re-quicken
        Where love nor spring-tide fails.

Sweep upward, rare musician,
    Thou courtly song-patrician
        Who never wanted grace!
Let others smite and thunder;
    Let man behold sweet wonder
        Upon our singer's face.

SONGS OF NIGHT AND DAY

LOVE'S TIDE.

CALM, clear and white,
Thou jewel of the night,
O moon of God, whose ecstasy is light!
My stormy self, a sea of restlessness,
Answers thine heart; and here I praise and bless
Thy pale and splendid arm of strentgh
That gathers all the eddies, and, at length,
In spite of winds and rocks and waves allied,
Resolves their discords in Love's rising tide.

O sure the faith, and strong,
With sun-illumined sky, or throng
Of clouds above, or surge within my soul —
Thou know'st that, hidden, yet thou hast control.
So, sweeping shoreward with pearl-laden wave,
My life-tide feels its gladness at its grave —

SONGS OF NIGHT AND DAY

Glad that the peace is all of thee
Who art my guide, dear ruler of the sea,
And gladder still, when on the shore of years
I cast some pearls made brighter by my tears.

SONGS OF NIGHT AND DAY

LINES READ AT THE FUNERAL SERVICES OF EUGENE FIELD.

NOVEMBER 6, 1895.

'MIDST rustling of leaves in the rich autumn air,
At eve, when man's life is an unuttered prayer,
  There came thro' the dusk, each with torch shining bright,
From far and from near, in his sorrow bedight,
The old earth's lone children, o'er land and o'er wave,
Who gathered around their dear poet's loved grave.

With trumpet and drum, but in silence, they came;
Their paths were illumed by their torches' mild flame
  Whose soft lambent streams by love's glory were lit;
  And where fairy knights and bright elves used to flit
Across the wan world when the lights quivered dim,
These watched at the grave and were mourning for him.

SONGS OF NIGHT AND DAY

Sweet children were there, and of every degree,
Who caroled his songs at a fond mother's knee,
   And Wynken and Blynken and Nod came to meet
   The Rock-a-by Lady from Hush-a-By Street;
And on toward the starry blue ocean on high
Ascended the children's sad, orphan-like cry.

"O, children's own lover and minstrel," they said,
"At length you have found here your own trundle-bed,
   Where, like unto ours at the closing of day,
   Your lips sing as sweet as they did in your play.
Dear Shepherd, who loveth so well all thy sheep,
Watch over our loved one who lies here asleep.'

Lo, as they went wending o'er roadway and grass,
I saw one familiar and sweet. Did he pass
   Away from the troop as they journeyed along
   With drum-beat and dolls and with lullaby-song?
Ah, nay; at their head marched with step ne'er so true
The poet's beloved one—his Little Boy Blue.

SONGS OF NIGHT AND DAY

"O, Little Boy Blue! and how came you so far
From lands beyond ocean and cloud-bank and star?
  Fared you all this way for your babyhood toy?
  Have you not forgotten our poet—and boy?"
He smiled as he moved with the children alone;
Then waited and prayed o'er his loved and his own.

"'Tis not a great change," said the Little Boy Blue,
"From heaven to earth,"—and he spake as he knew—
  "Dear children are there who have learned by his song
  That Christ is the Shepherd both tender and strong;
In heaven, there's nothing so sweet in our joys
As this, that we sing what we learned here as boys."

O faithless one, striving to scatter your fear,
This bard was no doubter; through sunburst or tear
  He sang such a song that the babe at her breast
  Passed thence with his mother to God's deeper rest.
Who breathes with these songs in his worship of love
May sing them again in the home-land above.

SONGS OF NIGHT AND DAY

There came older children with gray locks and white,
And near to that grave in the waning of light
  They thanked the dead singer that, 'midst din and stress,
When childhood was fading, 'twas his gift to bless,
And through all the clang and the dust-cloud of time
To utter again our lost childhood's loved rhyme.

And One came more near, who, when once crowned with thorn,
Enrayed the damp night till it thrilled with life's morn;
  His own heart was burthened for you and for me;
  His own blood redeemeth the whole world and thee.
He knew what true saving from sin's direst harms
Has gathered the children within His strong arms.

O, Genius of heaven and earth, even here,
In hours too much hurried for prayer or for tear,
  Thy voice once again o'er our tense-chorded strings
  Outbreathes, as our poet immortally sings:
"The kingdom of heaven is given alone
To them who, like children, look up to God's throne."

SONGS OF NIGHT AND DAY

Dear minstrel and lover, who, through two score years,
Found tears in our laughter and smiles in our tears,
   Dreamed you how the Christ, to the heart of our days,
   Did speak once again in your own gentle lays?
Philosophers falter, where, with your sweet trust,
We bury our poet's melodious dust.

Full soon o'er God's Acre the robins will sing
At birth of the dawn-light athrob with the spring;
   Their notes will be sweeter than ever, next June,
   When near your own grave they learn secrets of tune.
The meadow-lark's wings, when the wild flowers unfold,
Will flutter above you with music untold—

Untold, save to you, who, to harmony born,
By birth-right of poet, through midnight and morn,
   Found this ancient world of ours musical still,
   And scorned not its emptiest pipe to refill,
Till yonder, where bees, honey-burdened, will hum,
The pilgrims through ages to Hybla will come.

SONGS OF NIGHT AND DAY

What said you to Horace when Charon's lone boat
Came near unto landing, and, with his old note,
   He spake of the echoes that swept from your farm,
   And asked if your heart still was pulsing and warm?
Methinks you had laughter with poet and friend,—
Fine laughter, whose melody never may end.

Yet, far in the past, o'er the world Horace knew,
There lifted a tree that the earth's forest grew,
   And stretched on the cross, reigned the Christmas Day's King
   Who teacheth new ages and voices to sing.
The lyre of your spirit was strung by His hands
Who leadeth all children to heavenly lands.

Our Christmas is coming. How ever shall we
Have hearts leaping up with the old Christmas glee?
   We'll wait at the dawn for your poem and tale?
   That morn will be strange, and our good cheer will fail;
And Santa Claus, maybe, will just stay away,
Forgetful of us on the next Christmas Day.

SONGS OF NIGHT AND DAY

Marshmallows like yours will not grow on the trees,
Nor dinkey-birds sing over wonderful seas,
   When you lie there so still, and each waits for his gown
   To depart on the train for your blest Shut-Eye Town;
But the Christchild will come, and some time, after night,
We'll meet you at morning with Christmas delight.

SONGS OF NIGHT AND DAY

MIRABEAU.

AFTER READING VON HOLST'S "FRENCH REVOLUTION."

Unleashing storms that calm might brood o'er France,
Freeing the lightnings lest Truth's path be lost,
Mailed knight of Justice willing for the cost,
What prisoned noons hide in thy jeweled lance!
Voice of the age, our discord turns askance
To learn thy music through the holocaust
That, Babel-tongued, transformed to Pentecost
When man knew man beneath thy prophet glance.

Kingly with tempests, teach our timid time
What bloom of lilies grows when northern blasts
Meet rose-mouthed south winds on man's April plain.
Storm-girt are we—once let such speech sublime
Welcome the thunders while our old world lasts
To feel upon its breast God's gift of rain.

SONGS OF NIGHT AND DAY

ON LOOKING OUT OF THE WINDOW OF EMERSON'S LIBRARY.

HERE still he sits and waiting hears the pines
Murmur their secret and the Northwind sing.
Here where the robin in a hint of spring
Finds summer-song in untranslated lines
Left in his throat, e'en yet this soul divines
Runes mystic, primal, like the blossoming
Grown in the hour of life's first opening —
Still reads the seer the world's unconscious signs.

O for one moment when the silent chords,
Solemnly strung with harmony complete,
Once more may hold within truth's ample theme
All vagrant tones and all unuttered words!
Then midst the noise of life's accustomed street
Souls might find triumph in his calm supreme.

SONGS OF NIGHT AND DAY

SONNET ON BRITON RIVIERE'S PAINTING: "DANIEL'S ANSWER TO THE KING."

"AH, if 'twere true, how greater far than song
  The fact itself! An Hebrew prophet-seer
  Alone, unharmed, where falchioned Death flames clear
From yellow eye-balls burning in a throng
Of lions; and, through instants roars prolong,
  Pants with a blood-thirst, trembles at a tear
  Just fallen from the prophet's Israel dear;
Then crouches, snarling like a vanquished wrong."

'Tis true. What boots it, critic, thou dost doubt?
Open a soul's den. Ask Love's angel bound:
"Art safe?" Lo, crownèd Evil from above
  Listens, through compromise, to hear Death's shout,
  While sharp-clawed passions wander silent round,
  Dazed, cowered, and conquered by transfigured love.

SONGS OF NIGHT AND DAY

ON THE DUCHESS SFORZA WITH THE STOLEN CAST OF THE HEAD OF DANTE.

FAIR dame of Italy, thy scarf of green
Hides Dante's sad and lightning-bearing face.
Hold thou those lips of scorn! Thy kingly race
   Will sit midst gems and gold, yet may not glean
   The harvest-fields he planted 'neath the sheen
Of truths divine, unwelcome to their grace.
Mark thou the hour to be, when, in his place
   Of rule, some son of thine beholds that mien.

   Lo, this the hour! Thy scarf no more may hide
His lips of flame. Savonarola cries.
   'Tis Dante's Samson leads the foxes on;
   And, leagued with fire, they bring the furious tide
Scathing the world while a Lorenzo dies—
   A world whose ruin turns to golden dawn.

SONGS OF NIGHT AND DAY

ON THE RECESSION OF THE FALLS OF NIAGARA.

GREAT time-piece of eternity — earth's dial —
  Thou tumult-thunder of the clock of years,
  Whose diapason breeds a league of fears
That earth grows old and hastens to her trial!
One day the misty splendor hid the pile
  Of stone now long dissolved where man up-rears
  His city-towers, from whence his curious ears
List to thine anthem, sounding mile on mile.

So, strong opinions — erstwhile clouds on high
  From Truth's vast sea, then gathered into streams —
    Tumbled and plunged 'neath rainbow-colored bars.
In thought's wide realm the awful gorges lie;
  And deep, this side receding falls, still gleams
    A river's current mirroring the stars.

SONGS OF NIGHT AND DAY

AT BEACH ST. MARY.

The long brown arm thrusts out to sea
    A headland lost in sliding sands;
So Time indents Eternity;
    We live on Being's borderlands.

Man builds his lighthouse of Desire,
    Waits here to greet a coming sail;
Brings golden oil for Hope's faint fire,
    And will not let his beacon fail.

Here on the fronting height abide
    The prophets with their faith divine;
Here see they first the moon-drawn tide
    Tremble along Life's limit-line.

SONGS OF NIGHT AND DAY

Afar beyond, from shores unseen,
    Thrusts out an arm enflowered and strong;
And they who watch there hear, I ween,
    The same deep-billowed ocean-song.

And deeper than the sea, below
    Unmeasured calm or thunder-shock,
'Neath darksome mystery and glow,
    Firm lies the floor of hidden rock.

SONGS OF NIGHT AND DAY

ERYTHEIA.

READ ON THE ANNIVERSARY OF THE FIRST MEETING OF THE PARLIAMENT OF RELIGIONS.—COLUMBIAN EXPOSITION, 1893.

> "Erytheia, the legendary region round the Pillars of Hercules, probably took its name from the redness of the west under which the Greeks saw it."
> *Note of Matthew Arnold.*

NONE knew where the limit-line was drawn
   By viewless hands on the Orient seas,
Or where the West removed when dawn
   Swept through the Pillars of Hercules.

And many a sailor, with thoughts that burned
   'Neath a formless incense-cloud of faith,
Sat in his shallop and fondly turned
   To question the stars' resplendent wraith.

SONGS OF NIGHT AND DAY

Afar beyond where the wise ones said,
  Rose full on his dreams a visioned place.
Was it a home for the happy dead,
  Or the golden land of a nobler race?

A sailor is man, or a landsman thrilled
  E'en yet with a faith that sends its crew
Where he thinks the Orient waves are stilled,
  And the West begins in the fire-streaked blue.

There are wings that oft in the tranquil air
  Show bright in the glance of the morning sun;
They poise and flutter and vanish where
  The horizon flames when the day is done.

There are triremes sailing far away
  'Neath the purple clouds; and at night their oars
Dip gold where the moonlit tides convey
  Ocean to ocean 'twixt unknown shores.

There are Tritons, too, with horns of pearl;
  And far o'er the shimmering waves there sound

SONGS OF NIGHT AND DAY

To the mist-clad stars, when the waves up-curl,
   Such tones as from sea to sky rebound.

Melodious winds drift through the trees;
   Are they echoed strains of man's songs unsung?
For this is the soul's Hesperides
   Where the apples grow and the heart is young.

Never too high for the yearning hand,
   The wine-red fruit is forever fair.
The white-breathed frosts in this sun-girt land
   Kiss buds to bloom in immortal air.

These buds were hopes that had shriveled here
   In a common wind where the birds grow mute.
So full of June is that atmosphere,
   Each bending reed is a lover's flute.

O Man, are these but thy thoughts grown strong
   For a dream's emprise to the unnamed seas?
Dost thou breed such visions as ever throng
   Beyond the Pillars of Hercules?

SONGS OF NIGHT AND DAY

Shall never some wise geographer
   Set stakes where begins thy land of the West?
Shall thought disdain as a voyager
   A spot where the Orient ends its quest?

The mariner's dream of the East is true—
   "Sail west, my soul, to thy far Cathay!"
Man's thoughts o'er a sunset field of blue
   Sweep through the West to the East to-day.

Great truths transform, yet are never lies,
   Though East prove West, if we sail too far—
Who thought him to live as a sacrifice
   Makes soul for himself, finds his self's true star.

Quoth I: "To westward toward Faith's own shore
   Of citrus and balm for the weary mind;
Good-bye to Reason!" I cried—but more;
   True Reason in Faith is the goal I find.

Sunrise through sunset glows in sunrise.
   Westernmost thoughts ope gates in the East.

SONGS OF NIGHT AND DAY

At Concord lived Saadi; 'neath Occident skies
   Our Emerson sits at the Orient's feast.

O Christ, even Thou art highest and Lord,
   Master of Worlds and this heart of mine,
Lowliest one and most adored,
   Most human and near when most divine.

Ah, soul, thy world is an orb so large,
   Of circles so many and sweep so vast!
Forever thou goest from marge to marge,
   Yet never the Occident gates are passed.

And yonder where Erytheia vies
   With visions of life and love and dream,
Our fancies sail where the old day dies
   In the sundawn's rush of new day supreme.

SONGS OF NIGHT AND DAY

THE UNVANISHED EROS.

'Tis a time when the gods that are left us
    Are dreams sitting loveless and lone,
And the doubt that profanely bereft us
    Has melted the gold of a throne.
But hid near the sapphire-built portal
    There's one that looks younger this morn
Than when Aphrodite immortal
    Kissed Eros that hour he was born.

In cold and grey splendor beholden
    The gods, one by one, disappear.
Faith fears for her chalices golden;
    No more flames the sun's charioteer.
But out of the vacancy glowing
    One god comes as strong as of yore.
One Eden was lost us by knowing;
    'Tis Eros who bids us know more.

SONGS OF NIGHT AND DAY

Away on the mountains of wonder
    Are footprints that mark their retreat.
There's hardly a memory yonder
    Of gods who for long held their seat.
But where there's a heart with an ember
    Unblown into flames of desire,
This god comes through June or December
    And lends his sweet breath to the fire.

Why stayed he, though all the rest vanished?
    Why worked he where fades the last prayer?—
None know; but of everything banished
    Man recks not, if Eros be fair.
For love, after all, is so holy,
    Methinks this one god, having stayed,
Will bring the rest back to us, slowly,
    And man will not scorn that he prayed.

SONGS OF NIGHT AND DAY

ON A FELLOW-PASSENGER ASLEEP ON THE TRAIN, WITH THE POEMS OF BION AND MOSCHUS IN HIS HANDS.

Wake, wake him not; a book lies in his hands.
Bion and Moschus live within his dream.
Tired of our world, he fares in other lands,
Wanders with these beside Ilyssus' stream.

Dull, even sweet, the rumble of the train;
'Tis Circe singing near her golden loom.
No garish show afflicts his charmèd brain;
Demeter's poppies brighten o'er her tomb.

Now, half-awake, he looks on star-lit trees —
Sees the white huntress in her eager chase.
Wake, wake him not — upon the fragrant breeze
Let horn and hound announce her rapid pace.

SONGS OF ~~NIGHT~~ ~~AN~~D DAY

Unbanished gods roam o'er the thymy hills;
Calm shadows sleep upon the purple grapes.
Hid are the naiads near the star-gemmed rills;
Far through the moonlight wander lovelorn shapes.

Grey olives shade the dancing dryad's smile;
Flutes pour their raptures through that visioned stream;
Echoes like these our modern cares beguile—
Soft-whispering music from the old Greek's dream.

SONGS OF NIGHT AND DAY

ON HEARING OF WILLIAM WATSON'S ILLNESS.

"I am sorry to hear that Mr. Watson has been less well during the present week. The nervous tension which always follows upon publication may well have proved too much for him; it is to be hoped the relapse is only momentary."—*The Critic's London Correspondence.*

I.

No: not the sending forth his printed lines
   Has robbed the poet of his calmer mood;
But finding them along this life's confines
   Where mysteries within our knowledge brood.
He faltered first, not when he spake her name,
But when Truth kissed him with her radiant flame.

II.

Tense chords are his, and yet so fine that Day,
   Shining upon them for a lucent while,
Makes light too heavy; and what time his lay

SONGS OF NIGHT AND DAY

Outbreathes, let not his lovers speak or smile,
Lest their too urgent gladness smite his brain
And cheat the harp æolian of its strain.

III.

This is the price he pays, whose eager youth
   Has waited long upon earth's farthest shores and
     strained
Dear eyes of love and longing after Truth —
   This, that 'neath lightning-flash, the vision gained,
The soul's eyes ache to rest their happy sight,
E'en though the darkness deepen into night.

IV.

The poet's mind climbs highest; and his flesh
   Refines to filament of wonderment.
This bears him up within its wing-like mesh
   Until he grasps the goal of his intent;
And, holding fast the gain, his overweight
Falls through to flesh again, inviolate.

SONGS OF NIGHT AND DAY

V.

O what an hour shall be when, full withdrawn
   From that high tower he gropes in toward the stars;
He, fearing not its fragile steps, feels dawn
   Enswathe his soul unfleshed; and through broad bars
Of morning, long-wooed Truth herself shall say:
"Fear not; thou livest in unclouded day!"

SONGS OF NIGHT AND DAY

ON THE FRAGMENTS OF SAPPHO'S POEMS IN THE EGYPTIAN MUSEUM AT BERLIN.

I.

Red bloom of Lesbian apple-orchards wafted through
    long years
  Falls on these shriveled parchments like a rain of
    fragrant fire;
Yet burns not, save where Love's half-hidden palimpsest
    appears,
  Flame meeting flame, in rain of Sappho's tears—Love's
    rapt desire.

II.

If these be leaves of song, blown hither o'er an æon
    mute,
  Oft eddying with the æon's tempests—ever borne
    along,

How sweeter far the hour when green-hid boughs bent
    low with fruit,
  And Sappho read her love-lay, bloom and fruitage,
    all a song.

III.

If these be ruins of the gems crushed 'neath the feet
    of Time,
  Firm-chambered lights e'en yet to love-crowned souls
    illuminate,
Glints of her passion, fragments of a burning jewel-
    rhyme;
  What was the coronet she wore? O answer, shame-
    less Fate!

IV.

O'er these from Lesbos and her love-couch shine reful-
    gent moons,
  Grow thick, brown myrtle, starry jonquil, floating
    maiden-hair.

SONGS OF NIGHT AND DAY

Out of her heart-throb, quick and troubled, breathe
   æolian tunes;
Red oleander, love-emblazoned, tints the dreamy air.

V.

These be not vineyards on the hillside, clustered fruit
   and vine;
   These be not blossoms in the valley, gold of daffodil —
These are the red drops in Time's chalice of Love's
   wildering wine;
   These are the perfume from Life's garden Sappho's
   songs distill.

SONGS OF NIGHT AND DAY

A POET'S DREAM OF BELATED LOVE.

We two sat late at eventime
Awake at polishing a rhyme.
The apple-boughs dropped leaves of snow;
The goldfinch called his mate below
Our casement, where the moonlight fair
Shed silver on the springtide air;
And round me long white arms would twine
When Love breathed music o'er my rhyme.

Long years alone, till eventime,
Each worked on Life's old stubborn rhyme.
False pauses came; and music went
With every hapless discord blent.
Syllabic blunders wrought their way
Through weary night and vacant day,
Until, at length, at eventime,
We wrought together on that rhyme.

SONGS OF NIGHT AND DAY

O blessed peace of eventime,
Where long years melted in that rhyme!
And thousand tear-lit, loveless days
Poured all their unsuspected lays
Within the swelling rapture caught;
When thought was tune and tune was thought,
And thou wast glad at eventime
To help me set that shining rhyme.

SONGS OF NIGHT AND DAY

HARVEST AND HOPE.

WITHIN light tufts of yellow grass
    The winds of Autumn play and moan.
White clouds, like ghosts that change and pass,
    Fleck vale and mead, and then are flown.

Shy whortleberries, dark and blue,
    Hide in lone marshes wet and green ;
Wild clematis and roses, too,
    Blow on the hillsides just between.

In all the wayside's dust, and there
    Amidst harsh grass and in wan fields,
The goldenrod, with wealth to spare,
    The treasured ore of summer yields.

SONGS OF NIGHT AND DAY

The sunrise drifts among the pines
   And lingers on the maple-bough
So long, in crimson touch there shines
   His flaming word: "'Tis Autumn now."

The plover, flying southward, wings
   His way across the shadowed hills;
The brown thrush, musing sadly, sings,
   And sunset brings the whippoorwills.

The tall, dry reeds that pipe with tune
   What time the lyric breezes come,
Were erstwhile flower-crowned loves of June,
   Yet in their richer days were dumb.

Dear days agone, when all my world
   Of dream and truth and love's desire
Lay like a blossom closely whorled
   Within a soft green vase of fire —

Freed now by blooming, through the days
   Of summer sun and Nature's need,

SONGS OF NIGHT AND DAY

I blame not any strange delays;
   Life comes at length to be a seed.

Beyond the white and stormful dearth,
   Through snows and rain, comes fairy Spring;
Then autumn-seed will greet warm earth,
   And dear old birds again will sing.

SONGS OF NIGHT AND DAY

AFTER READING SIR EDWIN ARNOLD'S VERSES.

Give me red loamy poppy-lands this summer night,
   Let Lethe's stream flow soft 'twixt banks of moon-drenched rue.
Let me not waken in that paradise of light
   Where sleeps the bulbul with a waft of song — and you.

But let me dream and through the silvery pleasaunce roam,
   Where lemon-grass grows spear-like and the blue doves coo.
There may I pluck white lotus from the whiter foam,
   And on the rippled shores find peace and love — and you.

SONGS OF NIGHT AND DAY

Go with me, find with me the sun-bird's glowing nest,
  Hid 'neath a musky branch of amaranth and dew.
Shake not the leafage dense, but let us love and rest.
  I love your lute when silent, and your lips—and you.

So will we dream within the cloistered green and gold,
  Where sapphired wings are folded all the warm night through.
And when we wake enclasped in new love ne'er grown old,
  I will content my love with rest and morning—and with you.

SONGS OF NIGHT AND DAY

TO A DAWNING TALENT.

And was it darkness, only night o'erlit,
   Starshine mistaken for completed day—
That late dream-life wherein we used to sit,
   Restless, yet joyful, in our peaceful way?

Something has happened to our fitful sleep,
   Less like our sleep than like that straying beam—
O'er all the land and far across the deep
   Falters, then vanishes, a radiant stream.

New mystery abides in sky, on earth,
   Paler and smaller grows the best-loved star.
What strange and sacred sense of painful birth
   Clings to thy speech,—Soul, gazing near and far?

Morn! Is it morn? And dreams were not in vain?
   Ah, couldst thou not thy stars and mine keep fast?

SONGS OF NIGHT AND DAY

How, losing them, may we old paths regain,
  Find rest and solace in that fadeless past?

Never return? O friend, that world was good.
  Its mystery we knew with old delight —
What garniture of moonbeams o'er the wood!
  I know not this new mystery of light.

Within thy speech that trembled not before,
  What age-long runes more old than yesterday!
Like sea-shells, ocean-swept upon the shore,
  Breathing the world-wide ocean's primal lay.

Hast thou gone back to God, or comest near
  To God whose daytime floods thy lips with truth?
Where didst thou leave thy wistful boyish fear?
  Thou seemest old — thou blithe, reliant youth!

And nevermore shall we in calm rehearse
  Our chronicle of things and ways God made?
Nay! everywhere a bright new universe,
  And everywhere the night and starlight fade!

SONGS OF NIGHT AND DAY

I go with thee, and, mist-enfolded, trust.
   Surely the gray will yellow into gold!
Yea, these are gems. Last night they were but dust.
   Earth's self may be a star of wealth untold.

Speak once again! Along the mighty ridge
   Where paced our ghosts, are bands of crimson snow.
This is the day; and there a chorded bridge
   Arches the mist of waters far below.

Earth waited thee. These beads of crystal morn,
   Rondured in sunrise, were but cold and wet.
Speak thou! Say all! O herald newly born!
   My soul will feel at home in daytime yet.

SONGS OF NIGHT AND DAY

ON MOREAU'S PICTURE: "MAIDEN WITH THE HEAD OF ORPHEUS."

"After the killing and dismemberment of Orpheus by the Thracian women, his head and lyre were thrown into the Hebrus. This maiden has recovered his head and is about to give it to the Muses for burial at Libethra, in that grave above which the nightingale sings as nowhere else in Greece."

"And is it he? The Furies heard his lyre and wept
   The while he sought Eurydice and was undone,
When Proserpine was tears and Pluto's curses slept.
   Ah, move, dear lips, in whispered song — Apollo's son.

"Thy cheeks are wet with Hebrus, and I kiss thine hair
   That floated on the flood like wind-borne lays;
What time these lips of honeyed beauty kissed the air
   Abloom with melodies of sorrow-burdened praise.

"O Thracian women, whom slain loveliness may shame,
   My newborn love is hate for ye! I hear your scream

SONGS OF NIGHT AND DAY

That drowned within its horror music's heart of flame.
   Yet see! The full lips sing as in a glorious dream.

"Far up within the symphony of fadeless fires,
   Great Zeus hath set this lyre to quiver with a song—
Song lucent, full and free, to order all their choirs
   To music growing sweeter through the ages long.

"List! do they move again—these rose-lips touched
   with dews—
Not dews of death, but drops of harmony distilled?
Yea; for his loving shade her long-lost ghost pursues—
   Soon through her kisses shall his dreaming thirst be
   filled.

"Behold sweet lips that twitch with crying and with pain!
   They strain to cry so loud Tartarus regions hear:
'Eurydice!' and lo, blest face of peace! Again
   They move. Embrace her! Gleams thine eyelid with
   love's tear.

SONGS OF NIGHT AND DAY

"I give thee up, dear face! Let Muses bury thee;
  And there, when shade with shade ye wander through
    Love's vale,
I seek Libethra, love, and what deep melody
  Throbs in that twilight for me in the nightingale."

SONGS OF NIGHT AND DAY

THE POET AND THE SOLDIER.

A POET'S pipe lay lost within the wood,
And dryads came and played about its mouth;
Enamored breezes from the fragrant South
Wooed dulcet measures; then the dryads stood
To hear new music pour its gracious wine
Beneath a bower of rose and eglantine.

A hero's sword lay gleaming on cold ground;
Dry drops of blood were brown on edge and sheath;
And near the blade a ruined laurel-wreath
Lay rotting on a moss-grown burial-mound.
Beside them, robed in garments for the tomb,
Sat a lone maiden with a passion-bloom.

When wild and brazen throats of righteous war
Shivered the morning stillness with their cry,
And where the Right paused tremblingly to die

SONGS OF NIGHT AND DAY

At her last stand, a poet from afar
Filled the lost pipe with music; then a youth,
Laureled and brave, waved the bare sword of Truth.

O poet-soldiers, ye who sing and fight!
Nor pipe nor sword was ever lost in vain.
New armies form. Retreating o'er Time's plain,
Beside your graves they stand at last for Right;
And none may say if poet's pipe, or sword,
Win the best triumphs grateful years record.

SONGS OF NIGHT AND DAY

"THE SUN SHALL BE NO MORE THY LIGHT
BY DAY; NEITHER FOR BRIGHTNESS
SHALL THE MOON GIVE LIGHT
UNTO THEE."

I.

I LOOKED, and lo, beneath the verdured lea
The Day-god dropped his sandal in the sea;
And plashing in the crimson splendor, I forgot
The less enchanting duty of my humble lot.
Then, bending oar with oar, as on the hills his feet
Shone like fine gold in flames of furnace-heat,
I moved my shallop till it touched the sedgy shore,
Where, having done my duty, I could do no more.

II.

O God! and hast Thou heavens for my soul
Higher and deeper far, more stars in sweet control
Than ever shone along that path he trod,
Till, westering down, the doomed and vanished god

SONGS OF NIGHT AND DAY

Rose on another realm and made its ample dawn?
If *these* be mine, though sun and day withdrawn
Make mine eye sadder, yet I bid Thee take
All my old sky; so, for my soul's own sake,
Let me be sure of seeing God, when no more shine
Or sun or moon within that changeless universe of Thine.

SONGS OF NIGHT AND DAY

SIR PHILIP SYDNEY.

I.

This was, in sooth, the one whom poets sing—
  The tempered steel within a velvet sheath,
  The marble soul, so warm, a budding wreath
Grew on his brow and lived there blossoming,
Hero and bard, the eagle's heart, with wing
  Lustrous and soft, that on some clouded heath
  A dove might hide, till, flying underneath
The noon, each spot became a sapphire ring.

O Gentleman, whose dower of purest strength,
  Like morning-mist that made an old world new,
    Awaited noons to make it seem more fair—
Men bring to thee fond dreams of man. At length
  In thee their trembling colors chorded true,
    Stay—a loved treasure in our common air.

SONGS OF NIGHT AND DAY

II.

The age God made to make a gentleman
   Foretold him rich in texture, heart and brain.
   It winnowed eras in whose throes of pain
There pulsed a flower whose ardent lips began
To gather gold in Nature's primal plan.
   Within this lover's rhythmic heart and vein
   Moved the fresh youth of chivalry unslain
When God gave Sydney to His knightly van.

O large-souled age, with Shakespeare as thy child,
   Bacon thy nurseling, Spenser's lyre full-strung,
     Raleigh thy courtier, plague of popes undone;
In thee Time's heart, with straying chords beguiled,
   Broke into music with a song unsung —
     Then Sydney lived—true knighthood's bard and son.

SONGS OF NIGHT AND DAY

III.

Defender of sweet poesy! 'Tis thou
   Art poesy's most fair defence. An heart
   Like thine is lyric and a tuneful part
Of that full lyric God hath sung till now.
Thy spirit's breath is epic when the slough
   Buries our chariot-wheels, or when a dart,
   More poison-dipped than selfish care, may start
A league of doubts before whose scorn we bow.

That cup of water hath its fountains bright;
   And lips of bards, athirst with heat and pain,
     Have found Parnassian dew-falls in that hour
When Zutphen's battle-field was swathed in light.
   Whate'er may cease, here sounds one life's refrain:
     The noblest is the noblest in his power.

SONGS OF NIGHT AND DAY

EARLY MORNING AT PLYMOUTH.

THROUGH grey mist tangled 'midst the wooded hills,
  A brown-winged warbler, flying as he sings,
Stops o'er his grassy nest awhile, then fills
    The salty air with sweetness, while he brings
    Remembrances of vanished men and things.

I wait to hear him fill the silent vale,
  And know a soul has come again to earth.
Listen! Within his cell-like notes a tale
    Of sorrow! 'Tis a Pilgrim's second birth;
    Old anguish makes full concord with his mirth.

Here where his heart pours ecstasies of song,
  Two centuries ago, he loved and died;
Wandered with her the ocean-shore along,

SONGS OF NIGHT AND DAY

    And watched with her the starlit ebbing tide.
    Those lover-forms lie sleeping side by side.

Here now he comes with her to nest again
    And rear their birdlings near the self-same shore —
To know Love's joy of joys and heart of pain.
    Lovers immortal, having loved before,
    Somewhere this love shall nest forever more.

SONGS OF NIGHT AND DAY

POETRY AND MUSIC.

SHELLEY AND SCHUBERT.

Man's soul itself with songs of sky entrancing
Makes life a lyric field, bright dews enhancing,
Where lily-sounds in wild enchantment growing
Throng close, like stars, on vaulted darkness blowing.

ROSSETTI AND CHOPIN.

Far murmuring seas upon the white sand glistened.
Two full-toned souls for faint woe-accents listened.
When eddied passion's pains to calm were sinking,
These seized the concords, mate to mate re-linking.

SONGS OF NIGHT AND DAY

BROWNING AND WAGNER.

Thunders and whispers sway the jubilation;
Crashes of pains long past and joys from earth sweep
    near;
Then sobs and wails in rhythmic modulation
Breathe radiant, surgent song within a tear.

SHAKESPEARE AND BEETHOVEN.

What God wrote deepest in the soul is spoken.
Fair vase of tears and loves they brought unbroken;
Found every thread of secret joy or grieving;
Wrought out the dream, immortal mazes weaving.

SONGS OF NIGHT AND DAY

THE PURITAN.

God grew aweary of the rich low land
  That kissed the rivulets in banks of bloom.
God said: "I'll make me peaks of crystal, grand;
  And these with morning's glory I'll illume."

God saw the splendors of the meadows glow,
  And granted sun and rain to verdant meads.
God said: "Though cold and solemn, builded so,
  My rock-built heights be high as human needs."

God loved the gay, responsive souls who please,
  And, clothed in blossoms, scent the growing day.
God said: "I'll make me sterner minds, and these
  With shadow mark the sun's path on his way."

SONGS OF NIGHT AND DAY

And lo, amidst the beauty and the calm
  Of compromise, in long, compliant years,
Rose up the Puritan with sword and psalm—
  A stainless height, unclouded, without fears.

Afar the long gold sunstreak came and stayed
  Upon this summit like a crown of fire,
Filled all the gorges with the light that played
  With holy rapture of divine desire.

Deep were the seams that witnessed *how* he came,
  But fruitful all the landscape at his feet;
And always, snowlike, innocent of blame,
  His whiteness bore a rose-dream, world-wide, sweet.

And when God looks to earth for valiant minds,
  He rests His eye-glance on these solemn heights.
Here sleep the secrets of the stormful winds;
  Here stay and radiate immortal lights.

SONGS OF NIGHT AND DAY

LOST IDEALS.

SOMEWHERE within the treasurehouse of God,
  Where precious gems with primal glory shine
Walk to and fro, as o'er the earth they trod,
  Our lost ideals, radiant, divine.

I see them toying there with pearls and tears
  Once lost within the vacant world of Time.
I see them bending low amidst the years
  To hear increase of music in earth's chime.

I know not — are they brighter, dearer there,
  Than when we loved them first in happy days
When morning ran to evening with our care
  And o'er the earth breathed Springtime's roundelays?

SONGS OF NIGHT AND DAY

Ah, never fairer sight is given to men
   Than sprang completely bright before mine eyes,
And walked before me in the twilight, when
   The door stood open into paradise.

Sometimes I touched her with a finger-tip,
   And knew my feet went one by one with her.
Sometimes I straightened, felt her rosy lip,
   Then gladly called myself her worshipper.

My soul, make answer! didst thou look away,
   Or fall bewildered in her light sublime?
I only know I lost her. One sad day
   Vanished mine angel on the hills of Time.

No tempest blowing o'er the rocky height
   Disturbed the lustre flowing to her feet;
'Mid Life's commotion, in her calm delight,
   That loved ideal walked the heavenly street.

SONGS OF NIGHT AND DAY

In God's own realm, all beautiful they wait
   To make us welcome; joy is in their eyes.
Our lost ideals tend the heavenly gate
   And guide their lovers into paradise.

SONGS OF NIGHT AND DAY

THE CENTENARY OF JOHN KEATS, OCTOBER 29, 1795–1895.

WHAT golden wine is this poured sparkling forth
Within an hundred over-brimming cups,
Gift from a sister-century to ours—
Rich blood of grapes that purpled in full day
This side that fancied wall upbuilt by man
Whose thought alone divides the realm of Time?
These mellow draughts stirred sweet in tingling roots
Feeling their way 'neath fragrant leafy mould
That made a bower in Cowper's arid day.
Ours were the wide-leaved tendrils when the tide
Of vernal sap rose high and overflowed
In spray of whitest bloom; the vintage ours
As sunset splendor loiters on wan leaves
Beneath whose shade in latest Autumn time
Our century grown old sits with her past,
Bereft of Browning and of Tennyson,
Sipping rare nectar from her hundred years.

SONGS OF NIGHT AND DAY

An hundred years of Keats!—is this thy gift?
Nay, bard and priest at Beauty's shrine, 'tis more
Than one song-loving century may bear
Away. At this glad instant, when there break
Upon thy singing countless unnamed dawns,
Each hour of long millenniums crowds near
To beg of thee anointment and this boon—
That, in her songful hours, may reign that mood
In which thou sawest mysteries unclasped
To thee whose spirit yearned for Beauty's lore.

The poets come—new minstrels whose song-threads
Must fail to weave themselves in rhythmic dreams,
Till bards may know that Truth is Beauty's self
Disguised and taciturn, that men may love
Her sovereignty alone. Then shalt thou reign,
And once again shalt be the voice elect
Of that celestial spirit Beauty hath;
And, in high noons of thought, thou who art called
The Mage of Beauty shalt be known as Sage
Of Truth, and all most affluent melodies

SONGS OF NIGHT AND DAY

Will sink to rise within that harmony
Where Truth and Beauty evermore are one
According strict within thy lucent rhyme.

Not thine the shield of Middle-Age Romance
Agleam upon thy father Spenser's breast;
Nor thine the organ-pipes whose wave-like strains
Swept down from heaven and triumphed over hell
When Milton's soul, in Cromwell's time, was song.
Still less thine eyes found paths o'er fiery marl
O'erpaced by that imperial Florentine
Whose feet with Beatrice's found God's throne.
Not thine was Goethe's world-wide, human glance
That lit the secret mazes in man's brain;
Nor thine an Argive Helen's tale to tell
Accordant with a race's dream or doom.
These are of song's true masters; only less
Are they than Shakespeare—universal bard.
Yet, midst their winnowed chords, thy note sounds clear;
And as o'er leagues of time their accents float,
Each singer surer of the ampler theme.
Thy honeyed reed outpours its amber tones

SONGS OF NIGHT AND DAY

In sweet, delicious lyric o'er lush vales.
What time on mountain-summits these aspire,
Thou fillest old Earth's self with melody—
Old Earth our home, old Earth that is our grave.
Thou wingest even o'er her pain and strife
And makest sanctuary of her groves.
O'er her scarred bosom zephyrs breathest thou,
And from her woe there lifts the incense-cloud.
Let others tread the sphery provinces—
Thy spirit heareth here, 'midst dewy grass,
Such unwrit canticles as on white peaks
Grow mute midst loftiness and faint for breath.
Thou livest here. 'Tis well, when silence reigns
On starlit solitudes where genius lived,
That thou o'er earth's wide glades shouldst carol still
Of Beauty's new and immemorial birth.
In twilight hours, when other throats are dumb,
Breaks forth the song-stream of thy nightingale.

Thy brother Shelley's is the skylark's blithe
And soaring note; the nightingale's is thine;

SONGS OF NIGHT AND DAY

Whose plaintive rapture hides in mantling hours.
His were the stainless lips of gladsome morn
That, tremulous with prophecy of noon,
Grew vocal, and the radiant day was song.
Thy note, more dulcet, found half-chorded eve
Awaiting thee, and where, o'er Hampstead lawns,
The musing twilight weaves a tapestry
From noon and midnight, in thine age-long spring,
Thy spell divine the theme of Beauty wrought.
His was the cloud-wraith fringed with shining threads
His hand alone might snatch from skies inane;
His were exultant winds of melody
On lightsome lyre-strings hung in murky pines;
And man found skyey ways to tread with him
Above the many-languaged boughs that moaned
While Asia's ardor crimsoned snowy hills.

Thine was the lay of autumn, though thy spring
Scarce greeted May with perfect kiss of rose—
Autumn, whose heart with summer's throb of fire
In wiser mood goes hasting toward a seed—

SONGS OF NIGHT AND DAY

The pensive hour of swift transmigrant time
Enflowered and golden-leaved, fruitage of June
Made riper in reluctant love with frost—
The hour when life with birth is satisfied.

So, through thy consonant and o'er-ripe lines,
Mysterious winds besiege the tufted flowers
And bear them where, white-sepulchred in snows,
Blossom and verdure have blest burial.
His was the glory of Parnassus' mount;
Thine were the Hybla-haunts of hoarding bees;
His was the spear aflash with earthly dawn,
And thine the graven shield of primal noon.

Thy youth found altars where Greek marbles gleamed,
And, 'midst incessant London-fog and roar,
The secret of their fashioning was given
To eyes that Athens mastered with her calm.
I see thee standing near the splendid theft
Torn from the Parthenon and held for thee—
Thou son of want whose speech was minted gold.

SONGS OF NIGHT AND DAY

O, what an hour was this for Art's emprise,
When visions amorous of perfect form
Married Hellenic beauty to thy strain!
Thou hadst no knowledge of what sorrow comes
To days whose lights emotionless transform
Themselves to chambered systems hard as gems;
And men miscall them seeds when vernal skies,
Close-bending, ask for gifts to upturned loam
Of thought. Our haughty pride goes forth to sow.
We plant the furrowed soil with jewels dead
And irresponsive unto rain of tears
Or springtide sun. O, for one pagan more
So innocent as thou of questioning,
On whose white forehead, as on thine, are carved
No telltale wrinkles where life's cheer is lost —
One Grecian youth with joy's elastic tread
Whose offering is living seed of song.

Thine was the old idyllic trust in things
That smiled with Ceres when at length she fared
To Attica, and if thy joy was less,

SONGS OF NIGHT AND DAY

It only sighed in more delicious rhythm
When Ceres sat her down on that bare rock
Still called *The Stone of Sorrow*, or what time
Persephone, flower-laden from ripe fields,
O'erfilled a poet's measure from her store.

We visit Greece to hear a sage despair,
Or see a Socrates drain poison-cups—
For simple joy is alien to our world.
Thou saw'st Demeter's autumn-feast outspread,
And o'er fresh boughs and deep-strewn tamarisk,
Thou heardest ripples from the sacred streams
Up-flowing where shy nymphs concealed in caves.

Without our science, in its first grey hour,
Thine was the eye whose glance, like quickening Spring,
Opened the darksome mystery of March,
And led forth Nature's secret virginal.
Thou didst not pause to learn how far from slime,
Or yet how near to Plato, in Life's scale,
Was that blue blossom Cytheréa loved:

SONGS OF NIGHT AND DAY

Enough to thee that it was beautiful.
Let others spurn thy musky winding paths
And note how dreaming apes had hiding-place
And rioted within the moss and sponge,
Or some eye keener on the scent of him
Track Shakespeare's genius through long-buried realms
Of stone, or Chaucer's numbers 'midst the ooze.
Thine was the wistful eye to fathom glooms
Of night, and in thy song, to woo black buds
To ope their hearts. Dark questions came apace,
And man, with aching brow, went forth for Truth.
Still rose above the strenuous years thy hymn
To Beauty, glad with praise that Beauty is
And hath her own pure voicing. Even yet
That music bides o'er inharmonious times
From out whose night, with birth-notes in bright morn,
Fair-featured days uprise whose psalmists lead
The wedded twain of Truth and Beauty on.
Our larger-brained and heart-exploring bard
Who asked of earth: " *What porridge had John
    Keats?* "

SONGS OF NIGHT AND DAY

—Browning, the sage and soul-discoverer
For us who lost our souls within man's soul—
He feared not music might forsake man's brain
While he could hear thy chord-compelling rhythm,
Or see thy liquid light in unvexed streams
Flow softly on his tortuous ways. His song,
Oft stumbling o'er a rough-edged heap of gold,
Confessed thy melody and caught again
A mounting cadence from thy fervent lips.
And he whose faultless lyre made flawless song
Seem easy speech to lips in troublous days —
He whose strings felt in Wordsworth's wonder-psalm
The tones that moved his lyre to utterance —
He blent thy perfect music with his verse.
Thy golden pollen borne on charmèd winds
Dropped warm within white petals from Grasmere,
And Tennyson's full blossom oped one morn
Of modern poesy the flower supreme.

Dappling thy pools 'midst lilied nooks of song,
What purity of light! No stainèd morn

SONGS OF NIGHT AND DAY

Was thine, tossing licentious curtains back
Till sultry noon lays bare love's wasted heart.
Thine was the light whose raptures rise to noon
On Latmos' mount where young Endymion slept.
The wind that brought white blossoms in her mouth
Roved to thy lips and kissed thee unafraid,
And, when she roared about thee, thou didst say:
"She is my wife; my children are bright stars,
Beauty my king, and epic shapes his guards."
So pure thy spirit, thou didst vanish forth
In that voluptuousness of rhythmic air
To whose song-murmuring heart thine own was wed.
Thine was at once the fact and fantasy
Of loveliness. Pure beauty dared to live
And walk forthright, her vestal bosom bare,
With heart unwon since blithe Aegean days
Gave to her Bion and Theocritus.

Renascent Spenser's glorious Attic son,
The Phidian chisel calmed thy youthful hand.
Flowers blew upon thy path, and there attained

SONGS OF NIGHT AND DAY

A sculpturesque and lucent marble grace.
Love's lips, that for an hundred years have drunk
Their fragrant secret, are not wiser now
Than then; still seems this bloom alive and fresh,
As though they were not Beauty's chiseled forms.

Thou wast no craftsman, skilled to place thy phrase
'Gainst polished phrase, in crystal-circlets massed;
Thy passion breathed not choice mosaic-rhymes —
Thy tuneful heart its swift revealment made
Of that deep elemental rune which sings
Its way from artist's heart, through all he sees,
To art itself — the consummate response.
Thy craft was sculpture-song that, Orpheus-like,
Transformed immobile things worked on by thee
To wax whose texture stirred with hum of bees
O'er-burdened still with wafts of clover-bloom,
And so instinct with Beauty's latent theme,
That when once touched by thy melodious hand,
Itself became immortal for thy praise.

SONGS OF NIGHT AND DAY

WAKING DREAMS.

Between mine eyelids and mine eyes,
   Like red and satin poppy-leaves,
Lie soft the dreams of Paradise.
   They linger when my spirit grieves;
They quench the fever in my brain
And kiss my hopes to life again —
Between mine eyelids and mine eyes.

Between mine eyelids and mine eyes,
   Like star-beams melting into peace,
Drift on the visions out of skies
   Wherein eternal years increase.
I slip the sovereignty of earth,
And feel the light of second birth —
Between my eyelids and mine eyes.

Between mine eyelids and mine eyes,
   With Love's bright mystery and grace,

SONGS OF NIGHT AND DAY

My precious friends without disguise,
   With benedictions on each face,
Walk slowly 'midst the tress and flowers,
Or sleep within the garden-bowers—
Between mine eyelids and mine eyes.

Between mine eyelids and mine eyes,
   A wandering spirit, through my sleep,
Comes singing where the daylight dies;
   And tuneful founts of tears aleap
Begem the path her footsteps trod.
In hers my dim-eyed soul saw God—
Between mine eyelids and mine eyes.

Between mine eyelids and mine eyes,
   I live and conquer, see and know.
O let my spirit in this wise
   Along the trackless confines go!
No other universe is sweet
As this—forever bright, complete—
Between mine eyelids and mine eyes.

SONGS OF NIGHT AND DAY

CARE AND CARELESSNESS.

I CARE not that the storm sways all the trees
   And floods the plain and blinds my trusting sight;
I only care that o'er the land and seas
   Comes sometime Love's perpetual peace and light.

I care not if the thunder-cloud be black,
   Till that last instant when my work is done;
I only care that o'er the gloomy rack
   Flames forth the promise of a constant sun.

I care not that sharp thorns grow thick below
   And wound my hands and scar my anxious feet;
I only care to know God's roses grow,
   And I may somewhere find their odor sweet.

SONGS OF NIGHT AND DAY

I care not if they be not white, but red —
  Red as the blood-drops from a wounded heart;
I only care to ease my aching head
  With faith that somewhere God hath done His part.

I care not that the furnace-fire of pain
  Laps round and round my life and burns alway;
I only care to know that not in vain
  The fierce heats touch me throughout night and day.

I care not that the mass of molten ore
  Trembles and bubbles at the chilly mold;
I only care that daily, more and more,
  There comes to be a precious thing of gold.

I care not if, in years of such despair,
  I reach in vain and seize no purpose vast;
I only care that I sometime, somewhere,
  May find a meaning shining at the last.

SONGS OF NIGHT AND DAY

I care not if, a child in Life's high tower,
   I grasp in vain at many ropes above;
I pray to catch one dangling cord—for power
   To ring one note of God's unfailing love.

SONGS OF NIGHT AND DAY

AT SANTA BARBARA.

The long green leagues of open sea
    Roll shoreward as on yesterday;
The old lights shine on wave and lea;
    I hear the self same ocean-lay.

God! art not weary of Thy voice
    Set to such monochord of tides?
Soul! God doth challenge thee! Rejoice!
    Thou hast infinity besides.

With every mounting wave that bears
    White bloom of wide sea-meadows near,
I lose my dull brown shore of cares
    That binds my thought and spirit here.

SONGS OF NIGHT AND DAY

Gathered from out the ocean-noon
    That shines afar on stormless deep,
Made whiter by a silver moon
    That plucked them in their budding sleep,

The pure, translucent blossoms come—
    A wealth of splendor on the wave;
They bloom above my fears—and some
    Hide my unworthy triumph's grave.

And all around sounds strange and free
    God's deepest music heard in time—
The choral of eternity,
    In steady, psalm-like, prayerful chime.

This His divinest gift to me,
    To break my old horizon-line,
And challenge with Infinity
    Whate'er in me is yet divine.

SONGS OF NIGHT AND DAY

A WORD FOR FAITH.

The long-borne fagots 'neath my hard cold will
   Lie piled in order—yet are wet with rain.
I looked to Thee, and prayed—am praying still.
   Flame of God's love, wilt thou thy fire restrain?

Ah, Sun of Righteousness, art fled away?
   Are moon and starlight come to tell Thy doom?
Shall these transform, and, like a Milky Way,
   Lie like a dream across the vacant gloom?

Still I believe my fagot-thoughts are shine—
   Shine of the sun, packed close in warp and woof!
While I am man, this memory divine
   Lives in my doubt and of the sun is proof.

SONGS OF NIGHT AND DAY

Sun, thou art hid elsewhere, in iron and flint,
  When thou hast vanished and the day is done.
Strike I the darknesses; and lo, a glint;
  O kindling fire! O relic of the sun!

So, fired at last by love—old love so new,
  My work shall be the one acknowledgment:—
O God, I find Thee, doubt and darkness through;
  Earth knows no instant of Thy banishment.

SONGS OF NIGHT AND DAY

SEA FOAM.

Are they bloom of white on flowering waves
   For marriage of land and sea,
Or white-lipped hate that the shore enslaves
   And fetters what would be free?

Is the green that purples afar away
   The change of a love grown deep,
Or the charm of Love's declining day,
   When a love-dream fades in sleep?

Are the white-winged birds that fly through the dawn
   Great hopes loving sea and sky,
Or the ghosts of hope from a world withdrawn,
   Not knowing whither to fly?

O, my wondering soul, thyself art here
   In song and sob of the sea;
The ocean I see through smile or tear
   Is my portraiture of thee.

SONGS OF NIGHT AND DAY

CHRISTMAS, 1895.

THE bleak winds hush their wintry cry
And murmur softly with the sigh
Of Mary in the lowly place
Where shines the Baby's holy face.
Yet everywhere men ask this morn:
"O, where is our Redeemer born?"

The winds of time are still this night;
One Star is guiding calm and bright.
My soul, hush thou and follow on
Through day to night, through night to dawn!
Where childhood needs thy love, this morn,
Lo, there is thy Redeemer born!

SONGS OF NIGHT AND DAY

So, Jesus, with their carolled praise,
Thou comest in our day of days.
These bring Thee to our earth again;
We hear once more the angels' strain.
Blest be the children on this morn;
Behold our dear Redeemer born!

SONGS OF NIGHT AND DAY

A SONG OF WIND AND RAIN.

WIND and rain,
Away o'er the main,
Banqueting loudly with foam-lipped death,
And kissing swiftly with lightning breath,
Singing amid the straining shrouds,
Playing with life 'neath lowering clouds;
On from the Southland laden with bloom;
On where the summertime finds a tomb!
For wind and the rain hold converse together;
And wet sails gleam in the freezing weather.

Wind and rain
Away o'er the plain
Reveling gaily with rapturous life,
And bearing along in your wild, swift strife

SONGS OF NIGHT AND DAY

Harvests unreaped in the seeds you fling,
Autumns of bloom in the breath of Spring.
On, through the shine of an April sun;
On, till the winnowing work is done;
For wind and the rain hold converse together,
And whisper their loves in the stormy weather.

SONGS OF NIGHT AND DAY

A BOAT SONG.

    Sing as we float along;
    Sing as the tide grows strong;
And far to the wide, wide, billowy realm,
Borne swift and sure are ship and helm.
We are children freed in infinity,
When we sing and sail far out to sea,
      Till the day is done,
      And the red, round sun
Sleeps with eve in the rosy seas.

    Sing as we come ashore;
    Sing when the swallows soar;
And close to the fisherman's hut we glide
Borne swift and sure on the flooding tide.

SONGS OF NIGHT AND DAY

We are weak and helpless, but nearing home,
Let us gather flowers from the land and foam,
   Till the day is done,
     And the red, round sun
Sleeps with eve in the rosy seas.

BISMARCK.

Frederick's battalions, on whose side was God,
  Charlemagne's vast vision fadeless in the sky,
  Luther's bold protest, asking Fate to try
Stein's dream of order for the realms untrod,
In one supreme full sunburst o'er that sod—
  I see all these leave blood, and then ally
  The steel with truth, to speak through one calm eye
Their mission in the statesman's empire-rod.

"We fear no one," he said, "but God." Such fear
  Impels the German heart to sovereign cares
  And makes him servant unto God alone.
"*I must!*" he cries. "*I will*—let me not hear!"
  And so while that one calculates nor dares,
  Bismarck beholds and constitutes a throne.

SONGS OF NIGHT AND DAY

SKY AND SEA.

THE Harvest Moon from tinted skies
   The sundown left aglowing
Within the ocean purple lies
   Where silent tides are flowing

Afar on heights the dreamlike clouds
   Attend her in her shining.
The sailor here against the shrouds
   Beholds them while reclining.

The sky is but an upturned sea,
   The moon a ship of wonder—
Fair sign of that eternity
   That charms our souls up yonder.

SONGS OF NIGHT AND DAY

So seems the sea an upturned sky
   All fathomless, yet nearer
Than moonlit leagues where clouds float by —
   The upper sea's bright mirror.

Between the sea and sky I stand,
   The Infinite around me;
Round both is God; and there's the land.
   Let not my dreams confound me.

At Sea, September 9th, 1895.

SONGS OF NIGHT AND DAY

THE NAME OF GOD.

I.

ALONG the wasting mere of Time I passed,
Half-blind with introverted, doubtful eyes
That sudden searched majestic routes of stars.
My sight was strained—one instant's space
A microscope with o'erlarge glass; the next
A telescope too small of lens. Methought
To read that Name above all names men speak.
I called that Power enthroned o'er Time and space
On whose strange earth mine eyes were fading—FATE.

Till then my soul, self-pitying, had no woes,
But loved her fancied martyrdoms and sighed.

SONGS OF NIGHT AND DAY

One night came sorrow, unannounced and calm,
And struck within mine heart a place of tears
That welled up in mine eyes and bathed my sight.
Long days I looked not out or in, but kept
My doubtful vision in their soothing flood.

II.

Then Life spake: "Go, and look well to thy path."
I looked and I beheld not anything
So blesséd in my way, as this: *I saw;*
And hasting on to duty in that dawn,
I read there first for me the name of God.

I had but known four letters of His name,
F-A-T-E—of these the last misplaced,
Till in that hour's white light I found the whole
Of God, with sight made true by purging tears.
FATE throbbed with heart and swelled with holy love,
Till FATHER spelled Himself upon my speech.

SONGS OF NIGHT AND DAY

INSOMNIA.

So SLOWLY comes the morning o'er the world,
It seemeth somewhere in the spirit's dark,
Where, ghostlike, flap black wings of night-born doubt-
    ings—hark!—
Day's banner loosened once falls closely furled;
So slowly comes the morning o'er the world.

So slowly comes the morning o'er the world,
It seemeth somewhere in a dreamlit land,
The stream of Time were lost amid oblivious sand;
And where the ancient silver current swirled
Full slowly comes the morning o'er the world.

So slowly comes the morning o'er the world,
Till now a white hand reaching through the grey
Sets free my curtained soul; and jocund dawn of day
Smooths with bright-jeweled feet the waves upcurled;
And swiftly comes the morning o'er the world.

SONGS OF NIGHT AND DAY

LOVE AND IMMORTALITY.

Alone Love wandered through the dew and flowers
   Along a mossy bank where Lethe flowed;
And crocus-meads, 'neath trembling myrtle-bowers,
   Lay golden where the wan day's brightness glowed;
      And Love was fair
With pink-white feet and wavelike yellow hair.

Love sat him weaving coronals of green
   Enflowered with myrtle, sapphire-cups of bloom;
And beads of gold enwrought their velvet sheen
   Where Love himself had found his unveiled tomb;
      And Love sang sweet
The while the myrtle blossoms hid his feet.

SONGS OF NIGHT AND DAY

"I weave," he said, "these clinging tendrils fast
   To crown my brow when Death leads on his fears.
These seeds I planted blossom from my past;
   This mossy bank I watered with my tears."
      And Love was sad
The while the singing birds of May seemed glad.

"Kisses and sighs are these. My chaplet-crown
   Lives blossoming and beautiful for aye.
I leave my name in buds. Soft floating down
   The stream, Love's name will bloom alway."
      And Love looked far
Beyond the light of morn or evening star.

What time Love dreamed, Death slipped within the
   bower,
   Waved once his sceptre o'er the crocus-mead,
Grasped sudden, missed Love's crown of green and
   flower,
   Then lordly Love uprose, and, giving heed,
      His hand agleam,
The crown threw swift across the slumbrous stream.

SONGS OF NIGHT AND DAY

"Now to thy task, O Death," Love smiling said,
   "O river of forgetfulness, flow fast!"
A dream of life hung o'er Love's golden head.
   He cried: "O Death, thou canst not kill the past!"
      But Love had died,
What time his crown bloomed on the other side.

That hour upon that other bank there reigned
   A sceptered angel — Immortality,
By all his unforgotten yearning trained —
   Love's other self, or form, flower-crowned and free,
      And thus alone
Love, fleeter-footed, went to find his own.

SONGS OF NIGHT AND DAY

A BALLAD OF SPAIN.

I HEARD the clash of steel on steel;
I saw the glittering chariot wheel
Roll 'midst a cloud of dusty gold.
'Twas on a day in times of old;
  In Castilla—
  Blest Castilla!

I knew his face, dark-skinned and fine,
A rajah's boast of peerless line.
From out of Islam, flaming came
This Orient torch, to light the shame
  Of Castilla—
  Fair Castilla!

SONGS OF NIGHT AND DAY

A fleeter steed than mine he rode,
Pricked to his speed with shining goad.
But then my loved one, passing by,
Had caught the prince's evil eye,
      In Castilla—
      Sweet Castilla!

Steel flashed at mine, and tears fell fast;
What time the Moslem warrior passed.
"Come, come with me, his slave!" she cried;
And I rode silent at his side
      From Castilla—
      Loved Castilla!

And now I see her long, bright arms
Bedecked with Orient jewel-charms.
I teach her ankle-bells their chime,
And love her in this far-off clime—
      From Castilla—
      Dear Castilla!

SONGS OF NIGHT AND DAY

This day the vina-strings will sound
In vain; the prince will search around—
And through his tears the deep-blue haze
Will glimmer, when his eyes shall gaze
   Toward Castilla—
   Her Castilla!

And now two milk-white steeds await
The lifting of the palace-gate.
'Tis done! Die, prince! Without reply,
We speed beneath the starlit sky
   Toward Castilla—
   Our Castilla!

SONGS OF NIGHT AND DAY

THE PERPETUAL WOOING.

The dull world clamors at my feet
And asks my hand and helping, sweet;
And wonders when the time shall be
I'll leave off dreaming dreams of thee.
It blames me coining soul and time
And sending minted bits of rhyme—
   A-wooing of thee still.

Shall I make answer? This it is:
I camp beneath thy galaxies
Of starry thoughts and shining deeds;
And, seeing new ones, I must needs
Arouse my speech to tell thee, dear,
Though thou art dearer, I am near—
   A-wooing of thee still.

SONGS OF NIGHT AND DAY

I feel thy heart-beat next mine own;
Its music hath a richer tone.
I rediscover in thine eyes
A balmier, dewier paradise.
I'm sure thou art a rarer girl —
And so I seek thee, finest pearl —
    A-wooing of thee still.

With blood of roses on thy lips —
Canst doubt my trembling? — something slips
Between thy loveliness and me
So commonplace, so fond of thee.
Ah, sweet, a kiss is waiting where
That last one stopped thy lover's prayer —
    A-wooing of thee still.

When new light falls upon thy face,
My gladdened soul discerns some trace
Of God, or angel, never seen
In other days of shade and sheen.

SONGS OF NIGHT AND DAY

Ne'er may such rapture die, or less
Than joy like this my heart confess—
    A-wooing of thee still.

Go, thou, O soul of beauty, go,
Fleet-footed toward the heavens aglow.
Mayhap, in following, thou shalt see
Me worthier of thy love and thee.
Thou wouldst not have me satisfied
Until thou lov'st me—none beside—
    A-wooing of thee still.

This was a song of years ago—
Of Spring. Now drifting flowers of snow
Bloom on the window-sills, as white
As greybeard looking through Love's light
And holding blue-veined hands, the while
He finds her last the sweetest smile—
    A-wooing of her still.

SONGS OF NIGHT AND DAY

BETWEEN SUMMER AND WINTER.

I.

RED Autumn kindles on the vine;
The o'erripe grapes are swoll'n with wine;
September wails across the bay,
And, when the summer-scented day
Runs swiftly toward the sunlit South,
I see the red upon her mouth.
The berries linger on her lips
And crimson on her finger-tips.
    Ah, fare thee well!

II.

Come, kissing meadows with thy frost.
The firelight is thy Pentecost.
The Summer leaves the table spread;
Come, Winter cold, snow-filleted,

SONGS OF NIGHT AND DAY

And banquet on the branch and vine.
White priestess, pour the fruity wine.
The future feeds forever more
Upon the Past's immortal store;
    So, fare thee well!

SONGS OF NIGHT AND DAY

WHEN THE POET COMES.

THE ferny places gleam at morn;
The dew drips off the leaves of corn;
Along the brook a mist of white
Fades as a kiss on lips of light.
For, lo! the poet with his pipe
Finds all these melodies are ripe.

Far up within descanting June,
Floats silver-winged a living tune;
Winding within the morning's chime
That sets the earth and sky to rhyme;
For, lo! the poet, absent long,
Breathes the first raptures of his song.

SONGS OF NIGHT AND DAY

Across the clover-blossoms wet,
With dainty clumps of violet
And wild red roses in her hair,
There comes a little maiden fair.
He can not more of June rehearse;
She is the ending of his verse.

He waits, and, through perpetual days
Of summer-gold and filmy haze —
When Autumn dies in Winter's sleet,
He watches still those dew-washed feet;
And o'er the tracts of Life and Time
They make the cadence for his rhyme.

SONGS OF NIGHT AND DAY

THE COMING PARADISE.

I saw her 'mid the long green stalks
   Of silky corn in summertime.
I saw her 'midst red hollyhocks,
   And watched the sunlit pantomime.
For lovelier brown was in her hair,
   And silkier brown fell o'er her eyes;
And fairer than her garden fair,
   I saw a coming paradise.

I breathed with her the heavy musk
   Afloat upon the eventide,
And ran behind her in the dusk
   And dreamed I walked close by her side.

SONGS OF NIGHT AND DAY

Somehow the perfume stole my breath;
  Somehow the moonbeams quenched my sighs;
For there I kissed the lips of Death—
  Yet lived with her in paradise.

Next morn I found her where lush grass
  Lived specked with lilies white and large.
Ah, solemn clouds that pause and pass
  Afar from sea-green marge to marge,
Beneath your path I strain to see
  That one sweet face of all most wise.
Across a dark infinity
  Glows evermore that paradise.

At night the glow-worm held his lamp
  Against her forehead pure and white;
And down the green sward cool and damp
  She wandered, minstrel of the night.
I hear her often, when I tread
  The soft turf where they say she lies.
They count her name among the dead;
  Then flames my surer paradise.

SONGS OF NIGHT AND DAY

If, in the realm of amethyst,
   O'er plains where buds are blossoming,
Are clouds of gold or purple mist—
   I'll find her, in some eve of Spring—
Her lilied limbs asleep amid
   The glory where some angel flies
And stops, where softly she has hid
   My childhood's dream of paradise.

So, near her grave are hollyhocks,
   Red like her lips; and there along
The brooklet grow the tasselled stalks,
   And thither floats the robin's song.
That far-off perfume haunts the air;
   Wan moonbeams overfill mine eyes;
I dream, and fondle with her hair,
   And live again in paradise.

ARCADY.

BE NOT hesitant with me,
For I go to Arcady.
Winter is stern monarch here,
   And without the window there,
Scornful of the leafless year,
   Breathes his frosts upon the air.
Now from all the hapless trees
Every frisky dryad flees.
Be not hesitant with me —
Let us go to Arcady!

Be not hesitant with me —
Come, and go to Arcady!
We have drunk the Summer's wine —
   Every yellow drop is gone —

SONGS OF NIGHT AND DAY

   Plucked the last grape from the vine.
     Yonder woodlands hide the fawn,
Where, beneath the young moon's glance,
Lithesome dryads throng and dance.
Be not hesitant with me!
To the woods of Arcady!

SONGS OF NIGHT AND DAY

ONE NIGHT AFTERWARD.

THE earth tonight with Spring is sweet;
And once-loved flowers blow near my feet,
Because with mine thy footsteps fleet
Still tread with me this maze of time.

Mine eyes, so used to see thine own,
Gaze upward toward the burning throne
Where thou art blessèd; here alone
I'm wending through this maze of time.

    Mine ears were used to hear thee say
    What visions came on yesterday;
    And here I wait thee, while I pray.
    What hast thou found and known in heaven?

SONGS OF NIGHT AND DAY

How did the heavenly gate unbar?
Didst rest thy wings on what white star?
Or art thou near me, or afar—
Since thou hast found and entered heaven?

How fare the throned and happy dead?
By what dear angel wast thou led?
Hast thou my spirit's record read,
And lov'st thou me as I love thee?

Thou knewest doubt—didst sow in pain.
Do I sow chaff or golden grain?
O, once, as then, speak thou again;
Thou lovedst once, as I love thee.

How didst thou thirst for living streams!—
And thou didst find their shadowed gleams
E'en here. May I believe the beams
That fall and glimmer toward the sea?

SONGS OF NIGHT AND DAY

Is perfect sunrise, as we thought,
From out of flickering twilights wrought?
Didst find the noontide where we sought —
The full, pure glory o'er the sea?

Are seeds that ache here blossom-crowned?
Does every broken circle round?
Is justice true? Is lost faith found
Where thou hast been with God today?

Strike some tense string that He may bless!
Ask some strong angel to confess,
And let me hear the answer "*Yes!*"
From heaven where thou hast been all day.

SONGS OF NIGHT AND DAY

TWO TRANSMIGRATIONS.

I.

Four centuries before Rome's eagles flew
Above the blood-red crest of Calvary,
There hung above the seven white-crowned hills
The destined triumph barbarous Gauls had grasped
At Allia's encrimsoned stream, now bright
And flowing calm 'neath skies of sunset-fire.
The Tiber theirs; Porta Collina near;
'Twixt Palatine and Aventine they saw
The fleeing soldiers leave their city doomed
And hide themselves within the capitol.
Then undefended Rome went forth. The hills
Stood crowned with fading light of hope what time
The Flamen Quirinalis hid the jars
Within Boarium; and white-lipped men

SONGS OF NIGHT AND DAY

And women swayed the arched Sublician bridge.
Afar Janiculum lit up the gloom —
A torch of flame above a shadowed vale.
Pale, in that bright red hour of fear, swept on
Toward refuge vestal virgins in white robes
Soft-tinted in the dusky crimson glow,
When lo! Albinus hastened near, his steed
And cart o'er-burdened; wife and children piled
With coarse plebeian wares above the wheels.
His hour—the hour that linked a mortal man
With gods enthroned and Rome, o'erpassing love
Of woman or sweet child—the hour of faith
Had come.
        The Roman spake but once, with voice
Ne'er sweet to woman's heart, ne'er filled with love
Of child—the hour four hundred years too soon
For childhood's vision in Madonna's arms,
Or mother's rapture in the Virgin's face;
And soon the axle bore instead, a freight
Of vestal virgins o'er the crowded road.

SONGS OF NIGHT AND DAY

Fairer than sunset—only sunset days
Within her heart—a grey-haired vestal stayed—
Vestalis Maxima—and thus she spoke:
"Nay! I will perish here—be slaughtered first
With these defenceless; spurn a safety torn
From helpless children and a mother doomed!"

Finding a shelter for her new-made care,
She looked again toward undefended Rome,
Where, shut within the capitol, the hosts
Of Roman soldier-cowards hid their swords.
Swift as the flight of panic-stricken men
She met, the vestal virgin ran; and late
The closing day beheld her sitting near
Her sire—Rome's relic of a century.
The grey-haired daughter clasped the white-haired man,
Blind and awaiting death.
     "This last is mine
To do for Rome," he said. "I see not foes,
But hear them. O my vestal child!—and thou
To die beside me?"

SONGS OF NIGHT AND DAY

"Nay—protecting thee,
My sire! I'll call the wrath of deities
That never yet forsook the hills of Rome—
Gods, whom I met at altars, when, a girl,
Thou gavest me to holy tasks, will hear
My prayer. Hear now, ye gods immortal, hear!"

Serenely sat her sire—a senator
Stone-blind to all, save honor, in the hour
Of Roman shame. Like all his peers that night
The old man sat him in embroidered robes,
In death's auroral brightness, saying prayers
Of Fabius Pontifex. When morning came,
He mused within the colonnade, in sight
Of all; his only gem unfilched—this child—
Herself a grey-haired virgin waiting death.
His blue-veined hand held fast the sceptre white
Of ivory; and in his heart was Rome.

"Ah, tremble not, my child," he whispered soft,
"Would I had more to give to Rome than age;

SONGS OF NIGHT AND DAY

A shout, or stroke! Nay! even these are passed;
My life is now white-embered, wanting flame.
Would I might see thee once again! For now
Thou art more beautiful in face and form,
As in thy soul, than when I gave thee up—
That fragrant bud of mine, pulsing to blow;
And thou wast called *Amata*, yea, *beloved!*
O, like that radiant gold upon thy head—
A votive gift hung 'midst the lotus-leaves—
That shining past seems near, yet quite cut off
From all the rank green present blossomless—
I may but wait to perish with my child.
Hush! be they Gauls that shout? Nay, vestal, nay!
I saw thee once within the plostrum there!
Thou didst ride forth, the lictor just ahead;
And Roman consuls turned them, making room
For thee. Gods! Now, all unattended here,
Thou waitest with a senator, thy sire—
A prisoner of Gauls—to die! O Rome!
A monarch's life was spared on one request
The vestals made; and royal fierceness bowed

SONGS OF NIGHT AND DAY

To them. Come closer, girl! nay, vestal, come!—
By chance, a guilty wretch once meeting thee
Had his reprieve. And yet a brutal Gaul!—
Ah! heardst that cry? Their feet have crossed the spot
On which thou stood'st to sprinkle waters pure
As thou wast pure, when Rome upbuilt her fane
Of marble. Mars! Ah! Mars seems dead in Rome.
(Still must we hold to faith in gods supreme!)
Then thou didst guard the ever-burning flame
And Vesta's atrium made fairer still,
The while the loved Palladium was kept
By virgin eyes and Roman soldiery—
Hear, child! They clatter on the street!"

                                                  She saw,
And, statue-like, sat white-robed courting death.
A flame, bright prophecy of ruin, sprang up
Where erst the Via Sacra skirted close
The Atrium; and then a hotter flame
Burned white within a Gallic face. One shout—
And at her father's side she rose, the while

SONGS OF NIGHT AND DAY

A short sword, seized from death-chilled Roman hands,
Gleamed at her breast, then glittered suddenly
Above the senator, who silent sat
With all his peers—a long illustrious row
Of bearded statues on the marble steps.
The Gallic chief advanced.

"Nay! Nay!" she cried,
"Thou brutal wretch!" (for he had touched the beard
And raised his sword to strike) "Nay, Gaul! Strike not!
Strike not, till thou hast killed his vestal-child!"

Then, through his savage thirst for Roman blood,
There ran the soft sweet cadence of her speech,
The o'erheard voice of her who shone and stood
All beautiful. His heated soul, o'er-hung
With quivering atmospheres of Gallic hate,
Searched for a shadow in that blistering noon.
Within his bosom varying forces blent,
As, in some deep grey glen of bouldered rocks,

SONGS OF NIGHT AND DAY

The birds trill raptures and the serpents twine.
"Woman!" he snarled—and held the azure edge
Above her head, then saw deep eyes and quailed.
New thoughts grew fast, to shrivel in his wrath,
Like young green branches in a forest fire
That ooze with life and burn with furious flame.
There for an instant glowed a sunlike thing
Above the hard barbaric conqueror's head;
The ice-strong purpose clear and cold, shone fair
With streams of color quivering to its heart.
Then, hardening again, the light grew cold—
The blest ideal vanished evermore.
The man died out; the brute struck once, then once
Again; and Pulvius' thinner blood ran down
The steps. The ruddy streamlet trickled on
O'er mottled white, until it met the chilled
And sacred treasure of the virgin's heart.

Then flame was master, and the west wind swept
O'er Rome a desolation fiery-tongued
From Palatine to Aventine, the while

SONGS OF NIGHT AND DAY

The Gallic chieftain trod across the blood —
A blinded monster trampling hapless bloom.

At Curia Hostilia, when flame
Had died beneath the white-crowned Aventine,
The senate met; and Rome was eloquent.
One name breathed majesty and sweetness forth;
One name was foulest of that Gallic horde —
The vestal virgin's and her slayer's name.

II.
Swift centuries had gone o'er Rome. A Name
From Nazareth had brightened through the night
That led to daybreak o'er a moonlit world.
And there Time sat within the ancient walls
A-weaving moonlight in with sunlight-threads —
Night's leavings, precious wastes of radiance —
With first and silky threads of morn the breath
Of God had blown across the weaver's loom.

The ancient vestal's task was yet undone
That hour she saw the cross triumphantly

SONGS OF NIGHT AND DAY

Outshine the whitest temple on the hills.
She smote her milkless breasts, nor knew how sure
Through motherhood of sacred rite, one God
Would place her features in the Christian nun,
Nor, dreaming only dread, when, having knelt
Before the goddess Vesta, quickly rose
The last fair vestal in her snow-white robe
To look on purple-shadowed Sabine hills,
Full confident no Christian's sight might find
Her sacred paths or relics of her tribe—
Thought she how soon the underworld of Rome
From columned silences of catacombs
Should tremble song-filled with a sisterhood
Like hers—fair virgins worshiping the Jew.

The morning came to Merida alone.
The crucifix shone starlike in the dark.
With solemn murmur all the kneeling men
Urged through their clouded faith—*for Merida
Was foredoomed to the lion*—the voice of prayer.
A low sad rumor spread beneath their fear,

SONGS OF NIGHT AND DAY

And doubt lest God's care-taking governance
Had failed. Then outbreathed Merida, the nun,
Her own mysterious music. "I shall live—
And live forever!" Then the Christ seemed near.

On toward the amphitheatre she moved,
White-chapleted with flowers of purity;
Firm footsteps awed the thirsty pagan eyes
That hung upon her loveliness and peace.
Eyes lit with rapture of divine surprise
Swept calmly o'er the hundred thousand there
That looked upon insensate men who dragged
Red corses o'er her path, completing death.
Pure sunlight fell upon the silvery sand
Brought from afar to hide the streaks of blood.
Her milk-white feet had made a turning-path,
Avoiding half-chilled pools of blood, or splash
Of brown dry gore uncovered in white sand.

One rush of old remembrance dizzied her
What time she saw Vestalis Maxima

SONGS OF NIGHT AND DAY

Beside the Roman empress seated calm.
'Twas such a thought, like memory, as that
Of yesterday—the day her baptism came.
When o'er her rippling gold and forehead white
The sprinkled waters fell, the virgin felt
An old life thrill her brain; and pain with joy
Dwelt in her heart enthroned, contending there
For mastery of her. "O, once there touched
This head the waters of another faith,"
She said. And now she mused and nobly turned
And listened for some far-off angel-strain
Afloat across Soracte clad in snow,
Shaking the myriad hillsides as it came,
Blending its harmony with cruel roar
Of beasts, o'ercoming them with Christian praise—
Mused in the intervals of hope.

                                      "Lo, here!
This is familiar ground! My soul! 'twas here
I saw—or dreamed I?—saw from yonder place
Where sits Vestalis Maxima—saw blood

SONGS OF NIGHT AND DAY

Encrimsoning the sand, heard shrieks of pain
And saw, or heard, '*Police Verso!*' See!—
My thumbs went down. The red-sailed galley then
Bloomed roselike, moving slow on Tiber's breast,
Yet brought a lion; wives left couches built
Of ivory, to join the shout; and there,
Amidst it all, with royal, sodden leer,
Sat, olive-crowned, the Emperor! A dream?"

A long and vibrant roar filled all the space,
A green flame brightened in two yellow orbs,
The thunder shook the big brute's tawny flanks,
As out from damp and shadow, long denied
The freedom of his mountain-paths or flesh
Of tender kids, the famished lion came,
Awed by the sudden light of day and her
For whose sweet veins he thirsted. As he leaped,
He threw the sand behind him; men sat still—
For, midway in the air, he turned him swift
As bird or light itself. His outstretched paw
Pushed from his course the shining shape, but tore

SONGS OF NIGHT AND DAY

To whitest sand beneath her trembling feet
The thin white tunic on the virgin's form.
He ploughed the sand, and now the brute looked round,
And moaned and panted while he gazed
Where most the bright and amorous sunshine glowed
Upon the sand unrobbed of whiteness yet,
Where stood the virgin unafraid and calm,
And trampled 'neath her snowy feet the pride
And cruelty of famished Roman faiths.
A thunderous roar again shook earth and heaven—
In vain the powerless monster crouched to spring.
And then the shouts and thunder died away.
The air was awestruck at the silence white
That stood and reigned by right of purity
Within that wide-walled silence vaulted o'er
With silence, domed and pitiful as heaven.

Around her glory unabashed and pure,
The shivering beast went slowly wandering.
His head hung low between his thick-thewed arms

SONGS OF NIGHT AND DAY

That urged him close to her. His tail curled round
His leg, and crouching down, he licked her feet.

"I would not harm thee, helpless brute; quail not.
Thou art a punished soul; thy hell is flame
Of withering fierceness in thy cruel blood.
Thyself art leonine; yet thou art he
Whose stolen sword dripped crimson long ago
When I escaped the wounded body — pierced
So near the heart I lived in, I slipped out
The wound all bloodless, leaving thee to kick
The red corpse and my father's quivering flesh
Upon the stainéd marble in the street.
Look up from out the snarling brute, O soul!
For thou wast once a Gallic chief in Rome.
I perish here in Rome? Nay, death before
Failed thee — there, at the Forum's ancient steps.
Thou canst not harm me — thou, who art a beast!"

The while his hot breath warmed her marble feet,
He grovelled near, and mourned a lion's grief.

SONGS OF NIGHT AND DAY

Majestic agony inflamed the sunlike eyes,
That instant his uplifted gaze fell back
Within his sight from innocence so sure
And charged with lightning white as heaven.
No brute nor man dare look, and passion died.

Ah, hell is hell of fiercer heat for aye,
When next to heaven's calm, its hottest flames
Feed on themselves.

"Thou Gallic wretch!" she cried,
"Thy hell is this — thou must, yet canst not gaze
On me. My heaven this — I see my God!"
Still upward looking, lest she might lose all
In losing sight of God, the virgin fell
Upon the death-sick monster at her feet,
And passed from thence to other life beyond.

www.ingramcontent.com/pod-product-compliance
Lightning Source LLC
Chambersburg PA
CBHW020057170426
43199CB00009B/307